Still Here

Still Here

Poems by

Sam Norman

© 2019 Sam Norman. All rights reserved.
This material may not be reproduced in any form, published,
reprinted, recorded, performed, broadcast,
rewritten or redistributed without
the explicit permission of Sam Norman.
All such actions are strictly prohibited by law.

Cover design by Shay Culligan
Front cover photograph by Becca Norman
Back cover photograph by Peggy Burnett

ISBN: 978-1-950462-13-1

Kelsay Books Inc.

kelsaybooks.com

502 S 1040 E, A119
American Fork, Utah 84003

For Teri, Becca, Daniel,
and of course, MMN2 Benjamin E. Norman

HOOYAH!

Acknowledgments

I would like to express my sincere gratitude to the publications in which some of these poems first appeared.

Down in the Dirt: "The Big Dipper," "Fault," "Boots in the House," "The Majestic Theater"
Praxis Magazine: "The Screaming," "Broken,"
Verse-Virtual: "No," "Empty Sanctuary," "The Star," "Morning Fog," "Stained Glass," "Absence," "Colorblind"
Amethyst: "Hidden"
Red EFT Review" "Petty Bitterness," "Most Days"
Abstract Magazine: "Cracked," "Skeleton Photographs"

Apart from these wonderful editors and publications that have allowed me to share my work in their pages, I need to thank John L. Stanizzi. Without his help, guidance, and support, I wouldn't have even one of these poems published, let alone the book you have right now. Thank-you my friend.

All author's profits of this book go to The Ben Norman Scholarship fund. For any who would like to make a charitable contribution:

Coventry Scholarship Foundation*
Benjamin Norman Scholarship
Coventry High School
78 Ripley Hill Road
Coventry, CT 06238

*Checks should be made out to the foundation
with Ben's name in memo section.

There is not love of life without despair about life.
　　　　　　　　—Albert Camus, *The Stranger*

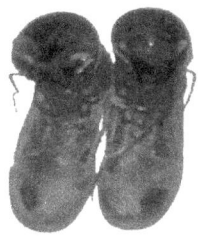

Contents

I. Morning Songs

Dancing	17
No	18
Boots in the House	19
Multiverse	22
The Star	24
Colorblind	26
Empty Sanctuary	27
Empty Sanctuary Part Two	28
The Light	29
Living Room	31
Morning Songs	32
Hidden	33
Dreadful Ignorance	34
Redeeming of the First Born	35
Stained Glass	36
Petty Bitterness	37
Dad	39
Big Dipper	40
Alone	42
Memory Loss	44
Fragile	46
Waves	48
Morning Fog	49
The Screaming	50

II. Absences

Most Days	55
No Waves	56
Absences	57
A Hard Rain	58
The First Snow	59
UNSLEEPING	61
Two Elms	62
Mystic	63
Still Here	64
Broken	65
The Majestic Theater	66
Fault	67
Skeleton Photographs	68
Fifty-Eight Thousand, Two Hundred and Nine	69
Anniversary	71
Renewal	72
A Spring Night	73
Driving	74
אֲהוּבָה	75

I.

Morning Songs

Dancing

At Teri's 50th birthday party,
a second chance prom,
I saw my parents dancing,
slowly shuffling,
the best my father could manage.

Someone was filming us dance,
panning from us
to Ben and Asia,
then back to my parents.

While it was sweet,
I couldn't help but think
that this could be the last time
they would dance together.

And I was right.
I just got the wrong couple.

Ben and Asia were dancing,
foreheads touching,
staring at each other.
They looked so happy,
so content,
so ready to spend the rest
of their lives together.

And they did, so to speak,
but not the way they planned.

No wedding dance.
No anniversary dances.
No daddy-daughter dances.

No, this one was it.

So they soaked in each other's love,
dancing slow,
with everything possible.
Unaware of the upcoming storm.

No

it can't be my kid
it can't it can't
my kid doesn't
drink
smoke
do drugs
is
smart
funny
has a goal
a fiancé
is generous
kind
loving
loving
loving
LOVING!
it can not be my kid
it can't be
it can't be my kid
God oh God
No.

Boots in the House

1.

Boots in the house!
Navy moms joyfully proclaim
when their sons or daughters are home on leave.

At O-three-hundred hours,
December 31st, 2018,
Ben walked through our door, unexpectedly.

He had driven 163 miles,
through the middle of the night,
after a twelve-hour watch,
to surprise his grandmother
on her birthday.

I was up, coincidentally,
and we ended up talking
and playing video games
until O-eight-hundred.

Boots were in the house!

2.

When she woke that morning at O-nine-hundred,
Ben's mom, Teri, bellowed,
Boots in the house!

Ben groaned and put
the couch pillow over his head.
At sixteen-hundred-thirty hours
I was asked to make dinner.
Ben set the table and we joked
about what a barbarian he was
because he put the napkins
on the wrong side of the plate.

Seventeen-hundred-hours,
we all sat down
for our New Year's Eve dinner,
the last one.

3.

We went around the table telling each other
what we were most looking forward to.

When it was his turn, Ben said, *I'm getting married.*
Shit, Ben, you win, I joked.

Because he had set the table,
he didn't have to clear—
so at eighteen-hundred-and-one
he texted Conner—*On my way.*

At sixteen-hundred-and-two,
Asia texted *Happy anniversary.*

And he was out the door.

4.

At eighteen-hundred-hours-and-nine,
the first responders found him.
They pulled him from his car.

He had broadsided a telephone pole,
and soon after was pronounced dead.

5.

His boots, which he had kicked off immediately,
for more comfortable sneakers,
are still next to the door,
toes facing outward,
next to the basket of laundry he was hoping
to do the next day.

Boots are in the house!

Boots will always be in the house
from now on.

Multiverse

A while back,
not so long ago
relatively speaking,
I wanted to kill myself.

I had a plan—three actually.
The first—I would drive into a tree.
The second—I would hang myself.
The third was to overdose on pills.

I picked out the tree,
I bought a rope.
and I had lots of pills because of my
diabetes and bad back.

Then things changed.

I decided that driving my car into a tree
was unfair to the tree.
I had also misjudged the height of my rafters,
so that would be a fiasco,
me stepping off a chair,
rope around my neck,
only to find myself standing flatfooted on the floor.
I also came to the realization that "death by Metformin"
wasn't going to work either.

Instead I went to therapy,
added an additional med,
and got better…
so much better, in fact, that I can't even imagine why
I wanted to die in the first place.

After the death of my son, Ben,
I was speaking to a close friend;
he was making sure that I was alright
and I could hear the unspoken question in his voice.

No, John, I don't want to kill myself.
I'm OK in regards to that.
His sigh of relief carried over the phone.
I'm just worried about you, Man.

At the doctor's office,
I could see the same question in her eyes.
Doctor, I know suicidal thoughts—
and I don't have 'em.

Neil deGrasse Tyson recently espoused
the idea of the multiverse—parallel universes
where each decision that each one of us makes
creates a new reality.
Somewhere there is a universe
where I get a call from Ben.
Dad, don't be angry, but I wrecked the car.

So, no, I don't want to kill myself.
I'm done with that.
I just don't want to be here,
in this universe, anymore.

The Star

1.

Each night since the accident
I have gone outside into the bitter cold
to look at the stars.
Some nights the sky is clear and brilliant,
the constellations dazzling.

Ben loved stargazing.
He would have pointed out
Cassiopeia and Orion's belt.
That's Gemini, Dad,
he would say,
and over there is the North Star,

Two nights after the accident,
Teri called to me
to come downstairs.
There in the sky was one of the most
brilliant lights I have ever seen.

Look, it's Ben, she said.
She believes in signs;
they comfort her.
"It's just a planet,"
I thought to myself,
and I went back inside.

2.

The day before his funeral,
we went to the veterans cemetery.
Stretched out before us
in orderly rows,
were the military headstones,
each one bearing a cross,
the symbol of Faith.
I said, *Aren't there any Jews here?*
Don't worry. Ben liked to be the first, Teri said.

And now,
when I see his star,
magnificent,
among the rows of crosses,
I know for sure that it is Ben,
no Faith required.

Colorblind

for Teri

My palette has been reduced
to a series of grays,
shades of black.

There is no room
for Prussian blue or Cadmium yellow.
My world is monochromatic—

muted mornings,
dismal days,
jagged blackened twilights.

I have become colorblind—
stolen is the brilliance of the sunrise,
the opulence of Coventry Lake.

These colors
were buried in
Veteran's Cemetery

when the honor guard folded the flag,
brilliant red, white, and blue,
that had covered my son.

Taps was playing:
I remember a hueless tune
in the bitter gray afternoon.

Empty Sanctuary

co-written with John L. Stanizzi

Love and grief hung in the air
of the empty room
like ground fog rolling in
on sunshine,
covering the frosted hosta,
reluctantly silencing the joy
of our youth.
And although their silence
is the silence
we hear when
they are gone,
their songs of honor sound
in our heart always,
sometimes like the sharp report of a rifle
in the winter air,
or the whispered breath of a lover
in one's ear,
each powerful,
each poignant,
each perpetual.

Empty Sanctuary Part Two

Last night I went back to the shul
to recite the mourner's Kaddish
where just hours before
I said goodbye to my son.
The auditorium was empty—
of chairs, of love, of mourners.
They, like people should,
mostly went back to their lives.

But I was struck by the empty room.
I wanted it filled again, forever.
I wanted to shout: *Do not forget my boy!*
His eyes, his beautiful eyes, his laugh, his wit
needs to be with you forever,
like it will be with me.

The Light

And if you feel that you can't go on
And your will's sinkin' low
Just believe and you can't go wrong
In the light you will find the road (You will find the road)
    In The Light
    —Led Zeppelin

Ben was struggling in boot camp.
He couldn't pass the running test.
But he learned to fold clothes and make beds,
to stand watch, and all the other skills
the Navy finds important for their recruits.

He just couldn't run.

We told him, *Keep your eyes on the prize!*
and *Hard work will be rewarded.*
We enlisted all the clichés we could muster.
And when he finally passed,
a week after the rest of his class,
he graduated and moved on.

In "A" school,
and in "Power" school,
two of the most intense schools
the Navy offers,
he was passing, but just barely.

We encouraged him!
There's a light at the end of the tunnel!
Joanna is waiting for you!
We are so proud of you!
We kept firing the clichés,
reassuring him,
trying to make him comfortable,
and build his confidence.

But now—
no more graduations, weddings, deployment plans,
no plans for a future.

And the clichés are different, too.
Everything happens for a reason.
He's in a better place.
God doesn't give you anything that you can't handle.
And I want to know,
Where is my light at the end of the tunnel?

Living Room

for Asia

We are not in a waiting room,
awaiting a call by the doctor
or the rabbi.

We are in a living room,
hurting and loving and holding
and moving into the moments of now.

Waiting for what comes next (or after),
can paralyze us, or worse.
We are trying to bank credits

in a celestial repository,
anticipating what will be taken
into a final accounting.

We must breathe and do what is right,
not wait for time with its baggage,
its unreliable measure, its poor judgment.

We are in a living room,
decorated with our deeds,
and surrounded by the living.

Morning Songs

In the dark early Coventry mornings,
where the only sounds are the fish tank filter
and the whistling of the heating vents,
the images come, unbidden, unwanted.

Visions of a rainy night, a sudden spin, a horrific crash.

Policemen brought us out of the hall
where we were celebrating the coming of the new year.
My wife collapsed when we were told the news.

No, no, it isn't him. It's a mistake, she whispered,
holding my face.
Relentless downpour.
Slick roads.
Our son lost.

Sleep haunted by that night, that moment—
The silence of the Coventry countryside at 3 a.m.,
the whistling of the heating vents.

And so I write these morning songs, these dirges,
usually maudlin and self-absorbed,
but there is no other way;
I must purge these images and sounds,
tear them from my memory,
push them onto the paper,
so that I can close the book at last,
and sleep.

Hidden

I have lost my boy
in a perpetual game
of hide and go seek.

I have looked
everywhere.

Is he in heaven?
He's certainly not
in the *other* place.

Will he be found
only in my heart,
my memories?

Is he simply buried,
a star above his head,
waiting for the rapture,
or for the rest of us to join him
and become stardust.

Dreadful Ignorance

It is been one month,
to the day,
since my son died.

At 6:09 in the evening
they found his car on the road.
At about 8:30, we were told.

So for about two hours
there was a state of being
where we didn't know.

I know, I KNOW that
we will never have him back.

But I would be willing to live
in those two hours
for the rest of my life
in dreadful ignorance.

Redeeming of the First Born

> *...Every firstborn of man among your sons, you shall redeem. And it will come to pass that if your son asks you in the future, saying, "What is this?" you shall say to him, "With a mighty hand did God take us out of Egypt, out of the house of bondage. And it came to pass when Pharaoh was too stubborn to let us out, God slew every firstborn in the land of Egypt."*
> —Exodus 13:13-14

Sabbath-
at the synagogue
to recite the Mourner's Kaddish,
which we will do, every day
for the next eleven months.

A young couple, reciting
the ceremonial *pidyon haben*-
hands over their silver coins,
redeeming their first born from
the birthright of sanctity,
the predestined status that their
child enters the priesthood,
back into their care, promising
to raise them righteously.

I flashback, twenty years
as I held my baby boy,
promising the same promises.

Siman Tov U'Mazel Tov!
The congregation joyously sings,
the couple's hearts are bursting
with joy and eyes are filled with
dreams.

I am in the back, the corner:
my heart torn,
gasping for breath,
my eyes filled with tears
and broken dreams.

Stained Glass

The world is a shattered pane of stained glass,
dull without the sun.

Shards scattered across the tiled floor defy repair.
I hope that tomorrow a piece, a single piece

can be refitted into its frame
and allow a sliver of light to restore some of me.

Petty Bitterness

1.

When they turn sixteen,
the scouts of Troop 25
go canoeing
down the Connecticut River.

It's a week-long trip of camping, eating over open fires,
a chance to spend time bonding with Ben, my semi-distant teen.

For practice we took our canoe,
old, heavy, and unstable,
to the beach across the lake
to pick up Ben's brother, Daniel, from day camp.

Halfway across I swamped the canoe,
and we were forced to swim,
pulling the cumbersome boat the rest of the way.
When we eventually made it to the beach
we lay on the sand, an exhausted spectacle
for campers to gape and point at.

2.

I spent hours agonizing over our equipment:
Should I buy the full fingered gloves or half?
What kind of dry bag is best?
Will this hat protect my freckled skin from burning?

At the logistics meeting, I announced,
I really like to cook, and I am willing
to do all the cooking on the trip.

Ben interrupted.
Dad, Mike will do it.
He's a really good cook.
I felt stung, but I let it go
because I was utterly excited to be going with my son.

And then the day before the trip—the *day before the trip,*
Ben told me he didn't want me to go.

He wanted this time to be with his friends
and not with me.

That night I went into his bag
and took the gloves I had so carefully picked
and hid them. I wanted his blistered hands
to feel some of the pain that I was feeling.

3.

I never forgave him.
I stopped going to father/son weekends.
I stopped helping to organize events.
To this day I haven't seen his Eagle Scout project.

Yesterday I found one of his rowing gloves
in the back of a closet
pristine,
unused.
I put it on
and sat down on the floor and cried.

Later today I will visit, for the first time,
the outdoor amphitheater
that Ben built for his Eagle Scout project.
Later today I will see what I missed.

Dad

My cell rang.
Dad.
For a split second
I was in an alternative universe.
It was Ben.
It was *Ben.*

But it wasn't.
It was Daniel.
And for a moment
I was angry that it was him,
and not his brother.

Then the wave hit hard.
And then the shame.

Big Dipper

Walking with Paul down the trail at
Camp Kirkham in a 3-degree January evening,
hoping for a clear sky.

I am here, in New Hampshire
with Dan, trying to help him heal
from the loss of his brother, Ben.
We are on a ski trip
with the Boy Scouts-
his friends.

I look up into the cold
New England night,
and there it is,
perfectly framed,
the Big Dipper.

The trees line the path,
and the big bear is standing
perfectly on her tail,
between the frozen limbs.

Ben loved looking
at the stars.
Paul taught him
the constellations.

The next morning,
getting ready for the day,
Paul holds up pieces of clothing
that in the past kids have left behind.

Somehow, improbably among them
is Ben's winter jacket, long lost.
I put it on; It fits me perfectly.

I am wearing the boots
that he hiked the Appalachian trail in.
His gloves, his hat, his jacket.
I am wrapped in my son.

Alone

> *And you know it's time to go*
> *Through the sleet and driving snow*
> *Across the fields of mourning*
> *Light in the distance*
>   —U2

1.

I wake up surrounded
by forty boys and men
in the Troop 25 mess hall,
packed together in sleeping bags.

I muffle my sobs into my pillow,
trying not to wake the boys around me.
I am writing yet again,
searching for reconciliation

where there can be none.
I write under my sleeping bag
so the light of my cell phone
won't disturb.

How can I be so profoundly alone
in the midst of so many?

2.

Later, on the two-hour drive home,
tears pouring down my face,
I'm listening to U2 and The Indigo Girls—
Lost friends and loved ones much too young,
So much promises and work left undone—

allowing myself to be shattered
in that way that only pop music can manage.

Alone this time—in a packed car.
The three kids in the back are blissfully unaware,
deep in their IPhones and Nintendo switches.

They have no idea that their driver,
the parent, the leader, the mourner,
is breaking apart right in front of their eyes.

Memory Loss

I was talking with Teri
the other day
about New Year's Eve,
the night Ben died.

Who got us home to Coventry? I asked.
We were would-be revelers
at the Elks Club, a town over
when we were given the news.

You drove. Don't you remember?
She looked at me worriedly.

I do remember the drive,
I think,
vaguely.
I was insanely focused on the road,
shutting everything else out—
when—improbably—a barred owl
swooped in front of the headlights,
and narrowly missed the car.

Oh yeah, that's right.

I went back to teaching last Friday,
probably too soon.
As the nervous, somber, youthful faces
stepped into my classroom,
I realized, to my shock,
that I didn't know any of their names.
I had forgotten them.
To muddle through the class,
I secretly referenced
my substitute attendance sheet

My God, if I can't remember
the names of my students,
or driving a car,

how am I to remember my son?

Already I am panicking,
realizing how few actual memories I have of him.
How long until those fade, too?

When he was an infant,
crying through the night,
I carried him in my arms for hours,
pacing around the kitchen island,
quietly singing to him.

His exuberance at the beach house
with Grandma and Zaide,
his rebellious teenage years,
his beautiful maturity as a young man.

These memories threaten
to abandon me,
to become unfocused, lost.
and I am afraid.

Fragile

1.

My daughter tells me that she has experienced
death sixteen times in her seventeen years.
Amy and Billy and Kathy have set her,
like a beautiful crystal goblet too near the edge
on the counter. Losing Ben has her teetering,
delicately balanced above the tiled floor.

2.

Teri speaks into the phone, her voice
dark and quiet. *I feel so hopeless,*
she says. Her ever-present optimism,
lost down winding Daly Road.
She looks at me, worried,
knowing my history of depression.
I don't know what I would do if I lost you.

3.

My son, hiding in a video game,
alternates between being a poor winner
and a poor loser. Cackling into his microphone
it is obvious that he has won this most recent
attempt at death and humiliation. The whole
family holds their breath, waiting for the
screaming to ensue.

4.

Cloudy, our pit bull, knows something is wrong,
something is different. She has always been an
empath, knowing when one of us is hurting.
Now she constantly paces, and pants,
and looks from one of us to another, trying to help,
trying to figure out what is wrong.
Her stress causes her to have a seizure, urine runs
uncontrolled down her leg, onto the floor.

5.

Everything looks more fragile, more easily broken.
Nothing is as sturdy or as permanent as I once thought.
I thought that there was some order in the world.
I was wrong.
Can I take the car to crew practice tonight?
My mind screams *NO! The world is too dangerous.*
Reluctantly I hand the keys over,
praying.

Waves

The five of us drive down to the beach,
late in the afternoon.

Waveside or bayside? Teri asks.
Waveside, Ben shouts.

For the next few hours
we watch the kids bodysurf,
joyfully riding the waves onto the shore.

But the waves are different now;
they are waves of sobbing, grief, despair.
These waves are less rhythmic,
less predictable,
but just as inexorable.
They threaten to drown me in my thoughts.
I miss him.
What a waste.
I am afraid, imagining the last seconds of his life.
Was he frightened?
Did he suffer?

One time, at the beach,
Becca got caught in an undertow.
Ben quickly, without hesitation,
grabbed her and pulled her to shore, saving her.
Officer Hicks, first on the scene,
tried to do the same for Ben.
But the waves were too strong
and now they threaten to pull us all under.

Morning Fog

In the early morning, before the day begins,
I imagine a world that still has Ben in it.

In the 3 a.m. Coventry-winter stillness
everything is possible.

But then the chickens squawk
making their pre-dawn demands,

and fog forms on the
vague, frozen lake,
and he is gone.

The Screaming

> *...I sound my barbaric yawp over the roofs of the world...*
> —Walt Whitman, *Song of Myself*

1.

Driving past each pole,
one by one in the chill night air,
those wooden fingers point up
(towards God?)
mocking me in their solid, straight, stillness.

Which one is the killer?
What should I scream at?
The rain?
The curve?
The darkness?
The Almighty?
The son?

2.

My wife lost her faith the last night of Shiva.

3.

FUCK YOU, GOD! she screamed,
as we passed another silent pole in the dark.
Please pull over if you need to, I say,
worried her tears will lead us off the road.

4.

I hear her whisper
I got nothing. I'm out of here.
And she is gone
before the service is over
leaving mourners, comforters, friends
looking confused.

5.

We drive home in silence.
Each pole reminded me of the
impermanence and hubris of life—
the arrogance that says
if we play by the rules
we'll be rewarded in this life,
and the next,
each pole playing along,
pointing up to where
we've convinced ourselves
we're going.

II.

Absences

Most Days

Most days I get up
and stumble through
the job, the study halls,
the meetings, the meals,
the Mourner's Kaddish.

Other days I stay in bed
reading and napping and
dreaming and crying and
struggling.

Or I float, sailing
into the ether, imagining
other lives, and other outcomes
living in a universe with *less*
pain, and (at least) one
fewer random
automobile accident.

No Waves

There were no waves today.

In their place, silence—
the thought of months,
years of dark thoughts,
images that sear, then
scar his memory;
a guilt that paralyzes.

I almost miss the waves.

Absences

Wherever I am, I am what is missing.
—Reasons for Moving, Mark Strand

I may look like I'm listening to you,
I might even answer.
But understand that
every bit of my essence
is straining
to be somewhere else,
in another time,
and that I am not here at all.

A Hard Rain

When the rain comes down hard,
like that night in December,
and Teri groans in her sleep while
I hold her hand and stroke her arm,
and thunder crashes, seemingly just
outside our bedroom window,
I count the time from the flash
to the thunder and pray
in the silence between.

The First Snow

The first snow fell
in the quiet
New England evening.

It's really coming down, Flip said,
getting ready to leave our house
after a day with distant friends,
(both by time and separation).

There is no wind,
just the gentle cold touch
of the flakes on my uncovered,
balding head.

Drive safely,
I say, managing (I think)
to keep panic out of my voice.

I say this to everyone,
regardless of time
or conditions
or distance.

Because.

The flakes are large and wet,
Instantly melting,
dripping down my neck
but starting to stick on the ground
turning the unrelenting browns and grays
to a uniform white.

A blanket,
I think ironically.
There is no warmth here.
Sadness, like the cold envelops me.

Please text me when you get home as I hug him.
I turn back inside as he walks to his car through the silent storm.
I shiver briefly and shut my door against the chill.

UNSLEEPING

More weight.
   —*Giles Corey*

As I stare, unsleeping,
into the darkness of pre-morning,
thinking of the could-have-beens,
should-have-beens,
the what-ifs,
I cannot move;
I am paralyzed by the mass of sadness.

But sometimes,
when the pressure subsides,
even just a little,
and I know that I can, in fact, get up,
I whisper into the darkness,
More weight.

Two Elms

Co-authored with John L. Stanizzi

Two paired elms, leafless,
their limbs stretched out
like the contrailed after-image
of fourth of July fireworks,
though the smokeless, noiseless sky
leaves us wondering
how, just a season ago,
the trees filled with color—
yellow and orange and red.
I walked beneath that sky with you
when the monumental clouds
were blue against the elms
and spoke to us of budding trees
and heavy fog,
of early morning dew that stained
our shoes and glistened
the way my eyes glistened
waiting for you at the front door,
imagining a sky full of reports
and unimaginable color,
the color from which joy is made.
Still waiting, the newly emergent
leaves curled, create a fuzziness
in the silhouetted trees, framing
an otherwise empty Avery Shores.
Rain is threatening.

Mystic

And when that fog horn blows I will be coming home...
—Into the Mystic, Van Morrison

I yearn to hear the fog horn—
announcing to the traveler:
Be careful! Unseen dangers ahead.

I will go, not heeding the warning,
step into the fog—
and lose myself.

I hear the fog horn blowing.

Still Here

It's amazing that as kids
we were indestructible
Scott and Harry and Neill
and Flip (who flipped his car with Amy in it)
and Jon and me.

We went so fast, behind our parent's back,
and took so many risks.
So reckless with our cars, our lives.
But we are *all* still here,

now with bills,
and aneurysms,
kids of our own,
alcoholism,
jobs, and divorces,
we realize
that maybe
we aren't unbreakable
after all.

And our kids,
so reckless with their lives,
because they are indestructible.

except,
sometimes,
we are reminded that they are not.

Broken

for Scott

His brain hid a tangle of arteries
the size of a softball,
and it finally blew.

He was forty-three and in a coma.
When he woke up he attacked an orderly,
so they put mittens on his hands
and tied his arms to the bed.

His sight was temporarily gone
but he recognized the sound of my voice.

Attempting to lift his head slightly
he whispered to me,
Help me break out of here.

The Majestic Theater

The Majestic Theater is abandoned.
Its gilded scrollwork faded and peeling,
the sagging façade in the midst
of a years-long collapse.

Inside are projectors seized and rusted,
next to stacked rolls of celluloid,
heroes long forgotten in the dust.

The velvet seats are worn smooth and shiny;
they're musty and moldy,
and the curtain droops heavily, aged.

The floorboards are warped,
slow wooden waves
curled by dampness.

Here the tide
is always going out.

Fault

on some socked in fault line
a light never goes out

terror lives there
even when we're together

we dig in our heels
refuse to budge

Skeleton Photographs

Seventeen-year-old kids
stare idly at the living skeletons
who were photographed
by men in uniforms.
The classroom is hot,
students barely paying attention.

The words that accompany the grainy
black and white photos,
describe men, women, children
immersed in ice-water
to test the effectiveness of
fighter pilot jackets,
or forced into decompression chambers
to improve survival for pilots
ejecting at high altitudes.
Subjects' brains dissected
while they are still alive
to test human endurance.

Dachau, where the doctors of death
removed the life and the humanity
of their patients
in the name of "science."

In the corner of the room,
two school girls are concerned
with what's for lunch,
their whispers drowning out the screams
of victims calling out
from the battered black and white photos
into the thin, foul air of eternity.

Fifty-Eight Thousand, Two Hundred and Nine

Standing in front of the classroom
talking about the Vietnam War
preparing them for the novel they
were about to read, I was drifting
inside myself, barely noticing my
surroundings, thinking about my
son.

When I came to the slide labeled
"casualties" I froze. Fifty-eight
thousand, two hundred and nine it
reads in stark white, 32-point font.
Fifty-eight thousand, two hundred
and nine knocks at the door. Military
servicemen saying the now-famous
words: *We regret to inform you...*
The same words that were spoken
to me at my door.

I imagine the responses varied:
anger and wailing and violence
and crying and dropping to their
knees and crying and screaming
NO! Did any other parent hug
the Petty Officer trying to get
the words out and whisper *It's
ok, I already know about my
son.*

Fifty-eight thousand, two hundred
and nine funerals, most of which
included rifles shooting blanks
in the air- the sound of taps playing

in the background, the color guard
slowly, carefully folding the flag
that covered their child.

Presenting the flag to their loved ones,
like they did for my son.

How did they manage the anger,
the crying, the denial, the feeling
of isolation, of being broken? How
do we manage when overwhelmed
by a car, a rainy night, the horrible
knock on the door.

A student says, *But I don't get it, why
did we fight in this war?* and I think,
back in the moment, fifty-eight
thousand, two hundred and nine families
asking the same question, *why?*
Just as I do, every moment, about my
son.

Anniversary

What would you give for your kid fears?
—Indigo Girls

1.

It's our anniversary. Becca said
One month, I think to myself as
I roll my eyes derisively.

Sixteen-year-olds have such a different
understanding of time. One month
is forever: a year, unfathomable.

They exchanged Teddy bears: Becca's held a heart,
his a basketball. He had also given her a ring,
which I made her give back because rings
were given for other things,
not one-month anniversaries.

2.

Ben and Asia are engaged
on December 31, 2017
and he presents her with a ring.
They are engaged one year
to the day, before the accident.

3.

Last Monday was his anniversary.
One month I think to myself as
my body shakes, my eyes

bloodshot from crying.
Asia asks *Should I keep the ring?*

One month is forever: a year, unfathomable.

Renewal

The coming spring
brings a anticipation,
of rebirth and renewal.
Spirits lifted, voices raised—
joyously.

Sitting cross legged
on a picnic blanket
next to Ben's new
marble headstone,
new grass sprouting,
I shiver slightly
in the cool breeze.

Rubbing my fingers
through the grass, I pray,
looking for my peace,
my sense of renewal,
which I do not find.

A Spring Night

Inspired by Boo, with love and pride

The twilight clouds hang low over the lake.
Muted conversation in the lake-side restaurant,
words barely heard, intrude on our reverie.

A squall, over the open water,
passes quickly in the stiffening breeze.
A single mallard bobs in the freshening
waves which lap gently at the rocky shore.

The duck, startled, flies away,
only the very tips of its wings
graze the water, once, twice,
then rises into the darkening evening,
leaving rippled, expanding circles behind.

As the sun sets, and the gloom deepens,
early season revelers step inside their lake houses
and vanish into the warmth,
silhouetted by a low yellow glow.

The air, smells clean and refreshed after the
storm, and the quiet sounds of the now-invisible lake
frame our thoughts as we walk home in darkness.

Driving

Power lines
parallel to the road
guide me home.

I turn right onto Route 207,
past a Tyvek-wrapped house
thrusting upwards from a mound of dirt,
like the perennials in our aborted garden.

Hundred-year-old stone walls
line Roses Bridge Road,
winding me towards Coventry,

where your parents' dilapidated summer cottage
leaned drunkenly,
boards sticking through broken windows,
a tree piercing the gable.

I have an old photo of a you,
a little girl, sitting on that roof,
when the cottage stood strong.

Years from now will we hold
a faded photo of Rebecca,
sitting atop our home?

I can see the water through the trees,
I say out loud,
alone in the car.

Over the speed bump
in front of Association Beach,
a family plays quietly in the summer afternoon.

אֲהוּבָה

"I am my beloved's and my beloved Is mine," – Song of Songs

Staring down the road
that is our future
is surely daunting, terrifying.
I can only hold you tighter.

But I am your beloved:
I can feel your love
and it sustains me.

And you are mine-
I *will* my strength into you,
through our grasp, as we walk
together down this terrible road.
This journey that no one wants to take.

About the Author

Sam Norman has been teaching high school for 16 years at Bacon Academy in Colchester, CT. He is an Aetna Fellow, and a CWP Teacher-Consultant. His works have appeared in *Verse-Virtual, Amethyst, Down in the Dirt Red EFT, Abstract Magazine, Big Windows Review, Better Than Starbuks, One Sentence Poems,* and *Praxis*. Sam lives in Coventry, Connecticut with his wife Teri, their children, Becca and Daniel, a bunch of chickens, their beloved dogs, Cloudy and Ripple, and newly found kittens, Pineapple and Posh.

Petty Officer MMN2 Benjamin Edward Norman 20, was involved in a fatal weather-related automobile accident early evening, December 31, 2018.

Ben was born on October 4th, 1998 in Manchester CT. Ben was an Eagle Scout from Boy Scout troop 25 of Manchester. While a Scout, he represented Troop 25 in Poland as part of their ongoing exchange with a troop in Krakow where he met the love of his life and future fiancée. After one year of college, Ben enlisted in the Navy, where he was selected into an elite nuclear propulsion training program, where he quickly progressed and was promoted to Petty Officer.

Benjamin had a real joy of life and surrounded himself with a group friends and family whom he truly loved. Ben is survived by his by his parents Sam and Teri Norman, by his brother Daniel and his sister Rebecca, grandparents Peg and Jim Burnett, Bonnie and Michael Norman, by his fiancée Asia Jurkiewicz, by nine first cousins, and many many loving uncles, aunts, and friends. He will be sorely missed. May his memory always be a blessing. Shalom.

www.ingramcontent.com/pod-product-compliance
Lightning Source LLC
Chambersburg PA
CBHW021024090426
42738CB00007B/891